Hushing the Voices

S. B. Lacroix

Published by Tenebrae Publishing.

ISBN-13: 978-0692535950

ISBN-10: 0692535950

Cover photo by S.B. Lacroix.

For Butch, the man whose voice
helps hush all the others.

Acknowledgements

The following were first published in
Shattered: A Collection of Dark Poetry and Prose
(AuthorHouse, October 16, 2009)

Autumn Regrets
Endlessness

CONTENTS v

"If I don't write to empty my mind, I go mad."
~Lord Byron

A Two-Dimensional Reality

Her words danced as emotion swirled throughout a two-dimensional reality. Mere words on a screen became a human heart, beating, ever fragile, yet persistent.

Rebirth

We die as we are born,
Alone—
Thrust into the unknown
And a light that is
Blinding.

In this world once
Known—
Prisons of flesh and bone,
Full of memories that keep
Lingering.

A Storm

She was lightning that struck in places that needed to be illuminated. She was thunder that rumbled what needed to be heard. She was a storm that left truth in its wake.

Nameless

I craved it
Like a drug
That had no name,
That knew no bounds,
Pulling the strings
Of a mind locked away.

I needed it
Like a road
That had no end,
That knew no traffic,
Speeding on the wind
Of a mind set free.

The Pain

She wondered if anything would stop the pain.
She expected it to rip her apart, but it held her
together with spikes that pierced her flesh and
made it bleed.

Bleeding the Blues

Blood flows from my veins. It smells like melancholy and tastes like despair. I cut deep because I'm not shallow. I'm endlessly trying to stop the hemorrhaging of a torn-out vein.

I spill blood onto my paper and wait. It has a story to tell. It has pains to purge. The blood separates red from the blues, the color of every shade of heartache.

Train Wreck

She felt it rip through her like a train barrels through a station it has no intention of stopping at. She wanted to shake it free, but it clung, infecting her with its insidious ache.

Shards of the Looking Glass

The shards of the looking glass
Cut me,
The mirrored fragments
Now scattered;
It pains me to see my reflection
In pieces that once made me whole.

The words have lacerated
My tongue,
The emotions have pierced
My heart;
I am bleeding rivers of remembrance
From wounds that refuse to heal.

Broken Pieces

She was broken pieces of mirrored glass in a mason jar filled with water. Placed on the windowsill, she would catch the sunlight and reflect it. Shards of reflective glass, she could cut or shine. She often did both.

Jagged

Jagged, frozen heart,
There was time
When it mattered

But I've slipped,
And I've tripped.

To its beauty
I was drawn
While it lasted

But time changes,
And it rearranges.

It was so cold
It burned
And I'm scarred.

Beyond Beautiful

He was beyond beautiful, radiating a light that engulfed everything. The darkness crept in and took up residence when he left, and nothing was ever the same.

Haunted

His memory remained nestled in the corners of my heart, lurking in the shadowed corridors of my mind, haunting me.

Between Love and Death

It was a death
Ever pending
Touched
By time

It was a time
Always waiting
Unwanted
By life

It was a life
Soon ending
Changed
By love

It was a love
Never ceasing
Unbroken
By death

Static

Letting go
And holding on,
You've not done
This before.

Lavender and chamomile,
Fields of eternity,
And you're
Running.

A freedom
So lacking,
A child
So small—

Will you die?
Will you live?
You've grown
Stagnate.

The Hazards of a Cage

She was a free spirit locked in a cage, but what a beautiful cage it was. Each day she'd roam about the roomy interior and look out past the gilded bars. She'd tell herself she was blessed to have such a cage, and perhaps she was. But she wept and she withered, for a spirit as free as she should never be caged, no matter how beautiful the enclosure might be.

Monday

Purple and pink flowers
Adorned my dress
In a garment that wasn't for day.

I had awoken to silence
And endless heartache
In a house that wasn't my home.

Each task I performed automatically,
Like a program with a mortal soul.

I had died, yet I remained,
Like a ghost covered in flesh.

Confusion of Consciousness

She woke feeling as if she had returned from another place and time. Her mind felt tattered and scattered as she tried to be present, yet the images remained. They whispered of the people, the places, the love and the loss.

Low

I felt the weight of the impending change like a led apron I had been forced to wear.

I had come to the edge of madness. I pondered how long before it consumed me and claimed me as its own.

Animated was I, this being of blood, devoid of the wholeness a person should be.

The voices would have their say. Their bodies consisted of paper, and they spoke with ink.

Again

Thoughts race
Through my mind
Devoid of calm
And I am manic
Again

The unease
Strikes my brain
An electric storm
And I am shifting
Again

Sorrow seeps
Through my veins
A black poison
And I am melancholic
Again

Of Ashes and Dust

The haunting wind
And its storm of pain
Swept upon me
Once again.

I danced in the darkness
With a broken mind
And a heavy heart
In a rotting soul.

I wept in empty silence
With an endless sorrow;
The obscured memories
Of lives once lived.

The ashes and dust,
Fragments of my soul,
Withering into
The eternity of me.

The Art of Dying

I can't find what I've lost. I'm not sure it ever existed, yet it keeps whispering my name amongst the noise of the day.

Over and over I repeat the same motions through similar days that turn into decades.

I'm growing weaker with each passing one. I'm fading like a dark fabric left in the sun.

What is life if not the art of dying?

Black nor White

Mighty bright,
Little light,
Emptiness have your way;

Starry night,
Seems right,
Darkness consumes the day.

Scrawling pen,
Remembering when,
Words I could never say;

Spilled ink,
Spirits sink,
Into the shades of gray.

Flowers of Heartache

It wrapped itself around her heart and
squeezed. She was filled with feelings that
seemed large enough to engulf her. She
thought that which promised to drive her mad.
She felt that which threatened to consume her.
She planted the flowers of heartache, tended
them well, and watched them bloom an odd
sort of beauty.

Visceral

Swirling in the belly,
Rising to the chest;
If you feel too deeply,
You will find no rest.

The pain that is screaming,
The ghosts haunting me;
The whispers of the voices,
My pen shall set them free.

Hushing the Voices

The only way to calm the chatter is to write it all away. Put pen to paper or fingers to keys, string the words and set them free.

Open a vein and let it bleed, the crimson offering that facilitates shall also appease. Be their scribe, simply oblige, write the words and hush the voices.

Madness is Silent

Instability, must you breed?
So be it then, plant the seed.

Insidious delirium, she said.
Insanity screamed in my head.

Madness is silent, I penned.
To meet reality, we bend.

To hush the voices once more,
Fetch the pen, close the door.

Kingdom of Insanity

The madness ruled, and she was but merely a subject in the kingdom of insanity. The queen demanded the contents of her head. She spilt them upon paper in a violent crimson red.

Unwanted

So much was taken
And equally forsaken,
I wish some could stay;

It was a passing, you see,
Just little pieces of me,
Slowly being torn away.

I reached as far as I could,
Perhaps further than I should,
My heart placed on display.

It might be easier, you know,
If I could just let it go,
But this gift I must repay.

Flesh and Bone

A sadness I couldn't put my finger on lingered
throughout the day, ebbing and flowing like
the tide, crashing waves of pain onto my soul.
Consumed by my somber state, I picked up my
pen and began.

Beauty will wear the shroud of darkness, yet
few shall truly understand. In a prison of flesh
and bone I wander. I see the unseen and
perceive that which has no perception.

The Feeding Well

From the well we drew
Those of us who knew
Melancholy runs too deep.

If it was but a word
We all often heard
Through us the feeling would seep.

And try as we may
It lingered throughout the day
And into words it would bleed.

Writing of sorrow and woe
With blood it would flow,
An aching hunger we must feed.

Daughter of the Moon

She came into this world ill-equipped for the likes of it. Scar after scar she acquired. Tear after tear she shed. She lived in a sorrow that swept her far out to sea. High and low with the tide, she became one with the moon.

The Shadows

I always went into that darkness. I knew the power it had and how the weight of it would pull me down. I knew the price I would pay for entering the shadows, but that was where the beauty lived.

Where the Beauty Lives

A feeling rises in my chest as it heaves with each somber breath, and I think I can't hold on.

My heart is drowning in an ocean of sorrow, and I wish this feeling gone.

I pace and I fret, but I can never forget, and such is my plight. Tears are spent as the night fires wane, and dawn consumes the night.

"This is where the beauty lives," a voice whispers to my weary mind. It urges me along, beneath the surface, to see what I might find.

I hesitate to relinquish my conscious thought, but know I must sleep. I descend into darkness surround by beauty my heart promises to keep.

Suffering and Sorrow

It echoes and vibrates as my mind plays each
one over again and again.

It creeps silently and it aches as my body
draws it through each and every vein.

It consumes and it destroys as my soul shreds
and the darkness rips free.

I watch it fill the air with its weighted presence.

It waits, ever so patiently, until I embrace it
and pick up my pen.

I listen, for it whispers, the secrets of suffering
and sorrow.

Unsettled

She watched each minute pass waiting for time to fade the feeling, but it lingered. She let it envelope her hoping acceptance would release it, but it persisted.

She sat silent and still as the night wore on. It remained, haunting her like a ghost that had no name and knew no life, but that which she gave it.

Too Much

I bled
Crimson compassion
In a
Foolish fashion.

I thought
Somber things
With such
Blackened wings.

I felt
An aching
Terribly deep—
Bone shattering.

The darkness
I touch,
It's always
Too much.

Bouquet of Melancholy

In the silent darkness she would gather the flowers of heartache. Vibrant colors of pain were their beauty. Their fragrance was of sorrow. She placed a bouquet of melancholy in water contained in an exquisite yet fractured vase. The fluid seeped through the cracks like tears, leaving a trail of wistful remembrance.

Spent

I made myself present
In all the places I wasn't,
And it left me aching.

I fed all those in need
While failing to nourish myself,
And it left me empty.

I died a thousand deaths,
Resurrected from each single one,
And it left me weary.

I existed but an empty shell,
Breathing yet lacking life,
And it left me not.

Possessed

It crept into her head and scattered across her brain flipping every switch it passed. It burrowed into her soul, infecting it with despair and snuffing out the light. It lingered in the corners of her room haunting her sleep. It took her form, black sockets in place of eyes, and roamed throughout the night.

Bitch

So this she said
With madness in her head,
And a heart full of screaming rage:

What does it matter?
And why should you care?
There's no need to act your age.

How they love to kick,
Their mean words stick,
I peel them off the page;

Green-eyed and lacking,
Vicious lips smacking,
Just to rattle my cage.

Tempest

I am the warmth of the sun and the cold of the darkness. How empty the space I once held will become. How my absence will haunt you like a ghost that keeps whispering all the ways you crossed me.

"They have no idea who they're dealing with," the one who fashioned me would say. It seems they never did. They mistook kindness for weakness, they took for granted, they used and abused. They loved so much they hated, and how intolerable such a twisted love becomes.

Push it away, and it will go, and how you will wish it had stayed. I never forget, and I never regret rendering what is due. When my tolerance is at its end, the winds shall increase and it shall be unleashed—that is the day they rue.

Satisfy Your Greed

What do you expect from me?
How much would you like me to bleed?
Shall I open a vein till I'm near death?
Will that satisfy your greed?

I could bleed you a bloody river
And you would still expect more;
All the cards played are hearts
And you're always keeping score.

Love is your weapon of choice,
Blood soaked spear and sword;
The river of my blood keeps flowing,
Like rain its crimson has poured.

You've gotten what you wanted,
Yet I am still expected to bleed;
Opened a vein and I'm near death,
There's no satisfying your greed.

Marked

She had scars that would never fade, and she thought maybe it was better that way. They were distorted flesh that whispered the names of those who caused them, like tattoos of pain, a reminder that some love isn't love at all.

The Red Door

It wasn't but once,
You thought it was twice,
In a row of burning flames;

You're no good at this,
Overly sensitive and deep,
A prisoner to these games.

The sound of those years
Echo in your head,
Yet you want them more;

I can't follow you again
Into the world you create
Kept behind the red door.

The Door of Paper and Ink

I swept so many things I could never say under the carpet, and I kept tripping over the rug covered lumps. I bit my tongue often, the taste of blood familiar, but my pen would not be still.

The blood I had tasted would seep out my veins and spill onto paper, helping to quiet the chatter in my head. It would give the ghosts littering the hallways of my mind a way out through a door that would keep me sane, a door that would free the memories and hush the voices, a door created with paper and ink.

Mettle

It comes and
It goes
I can't
Tell you why
The nature
Of things is
Everything must die.

Rip from me
My heart
A gift
I cannot repay
Tear from me
My will
For it cannot stay.

It's not easy
To understand
Some things
Aren't right
Never
Go down
Without a fight.

Morning Melancholy

I awake to find the madness flittering about my head, each synapse in my brain as squirrelly as the rodent in my backyard raiding the bird feeder. Each manic thought ravages my recently-returned-to-consciousness state of mind. The unease it brings is nearly intolerable, and quickly becomes a fire that must be snuffed out.

I roam around the kitchen, swallowing medication, considering food, but only managing a glass of fizzy water as the storm rages within. It pushes me around like a bully in a schoolyard until eventually I fall, and the blanket of melancholia wraps itself around me.

I hear a voice that assures me this is better— this heavy sadness—than the rattling of the manic madness that slowly suffocates under the weight of this blanket of sorrow. I want to believe it. I want to think it has come to help me, but I know it is simply the other side of a coin I can never manage to lose.

Emptiness creeps in, taking its stabbing path, entering my veins like poison. It spreads its sadness, its insidious ache. It grows, transforming itself into a large void that cannot be filled, and I have fallen through it like a black hole in space.

I look around my kitchen. Nothing has changed. Everything is in its place, yet I am not the same person who stood at the window watching a squirrel eat sunflower seeds as my mind unraveled.

Morning melancholy has found me again. It has given me its dark gifts of what it considers comfort. My thoughts slow. My body becomes laden with the burdens of my mind, and their weight is cumbersome.

I am alone in the depths of my soul and it is dark indeed. Each day I awake and enter my prison. While it is ever familiar, I never get used to it. I persist despite it. I revolt to spite it. I fight to break free.

Sew

I wept for all the things I could never say, torn in ways that could never be mended, even with the best needle and thread.

I was beautifully scarred and pathetically disfigured. I was a rotting corpse full of butterflies of colors barely imaginable.

I abandoned all that I never was. I released all that I would never possess.

I hoped death was like night eternal, endlessly peaceful, with the sound of a strong wind through the trees.

Autumn Regrets

As I walked a path of orange and gold,
The crisp feeling of the autumn air;
I found myself lost in the memory of you,
And pondered how life was unfair.

I closed my eyes and took a deep breath,
Had I come to terms with my choice?
Sorrow washed in and filled me with regret;
In my mind echoes the sound of your voice.

The sunlight faded, the days grew short,
Had I wasted time or had it slipped away?
I watched my feet as they rustled the leaves;
A somber emptiness consumed me that day.

Becoming October

She felt tattered. Pieces of her soul were
everywhere, and she could not gather them all.
She watched as they scattered in the wind,
caught on tree branches, and swirled with the
fallen leaves.

Moth Eaten

She didn't know every pain, but she knew how it ate holes in your soul like a moth with a wool sweater. She would have stopped the pain if she could, but understood it had its purpose, even if one could make no sense of it at all.

The Door to Madness

There will be no end to this if I don't empty my thoughts onto paper. It is both freedom and prison. I struggle between the two.

The pain is paralyzing. I would give in to tears, but they are long gone. They spilled their salty souls from the windows to mine and left me with an aching head. The cowards deserted me and left me to drown in these thoughts and feelings.

And this is the door to madness. I know it is. I've seen it before. Sleep must soon be sought or death will become appealing.

It is quiet, as am I. The only sounds are the clicking of the keyboard, the *tick-tock* of the pendulum, and the grinding of my teeth. I fear if I were to allow my mouth to open, I would scream, and that would signal the opening of the door, like some ghoulish alarm.

The cowards suddenly return. They again spill their salty souls from the windows to mine just before my mind cracks. The thoughts have been emptied; the feelings released. Through vision blurred with tears, I watch as the door fades.

Another Day in Paradise

Wind chimes danced and sang in the warm breeze as heartstrings broke. The sunlight slipped into the shadowed corners exposing the ghosts. They ran into the shade of the trees whose leaves whispered ancient secrets. The inviting body of water just off the back deck soothed all the pains of the day as it faded away, pulling her under.

Restart

Swimming in clear
Cool water,
Drifting to
A place
I'd once been;

Empty and full
Of everything
And nothing,
Slowly drowning.

Breathe the water,
Fill the lungs
With life,
Less air—
Another beginning.

The Traveler's Promise

Take the dusty road
And I'll take your hand—
Miles and miles to somewhere;

It's not that easy
To run from the past—
Years and years to nowhere.

If you'd just let it be
And learn to forget—
Layers and layers of nothing;

We could leave this place
And I'd show you the world—
Time and time of something.

Storm of Madness

The storm is raging once again. I could pretend it's not happening, but we both know it doesn't work that way.

The day I walked the path, I was a visitor there. I told you I know things I don't want to know. I wish it wasn't this way.

Meet me in the tree grove, and tell me why it doesn't matter anymore. Show me the door to the place we've been before.

Take my hand and walk with me. Tell me your secrets again. Bring me back to reality.

Magic Man

He took up residence in my heart. He showed its bruised beat a radiant rhythm. He had that way about him. He fixed what was broken. He made everything better. He had no idea the power he possessed.

Perfect

He knew my darkest secrets. He knew my worst fears. He knew how utterly damaged I was, yet he loved me as if I were perfect.

Buried

It seemed as if I were motionless as I walked. The walls of the hallway disappeared. He was like a light guiding me. Transfixed by his radiance, I couldn't look away.

It possessed me, and I could not resist. I touched him, and in that brief contact I was hooked. He was my favorite drug. He was the best high. He was the best low.

I cut myself, and he bled. I loved its crimson glow. I spilled more than I should.

I buried him in my heart.

Seamlessly

She loved with a force that left her heart
fracture. It remained in pieces rattling around
in her chest until she met him. Piece by piece
he put it together almost seamlessly.

One

Theirs was a love time could not touch. It existed before it had begun, and it would remain after it ended.

Theirs was a bond few knew. It preceded life, and it transcended death.

Theirs was a soul that divided, each entering a vessel of flesh and bone, each seeking its other half from the first breath.

Unending

She began where he ended. She often
wondered where that was. He left each
morning and returned each night, as did her
heart. The hours in between left her chest
empty, filled with nothing but the sounds of
her breath, and the ache of longing.

The Beautifully Bled

He was the color of melancholy and the scent of heartache. He felt like worn velvet and looked like fractured quartz. He sounded like the night sky. He gave until it hurt. He bled so beautifully.

Otherworldly

She always looked as if she were lost between this world and another. Her eyes were the color of yearning. Her heartbeat was the rhythm of regret. Her thoughts were from another time. They were holding her space in a place she did not belong.

Every Illusion

I lost my way on a path that wasn't there.
I forgot my name in a place I didn't belong.
I couldn't see—the light was so bright. I
wouldn't remember—the pain was so
consuming. As intoxicatingly beautiful and
inviting the field of poppies may be, I could
never submit to their mind-numbing sleep.

Alien

They didn't understand her. They expected her
to be like them. They applied pressure, but she
wouldn't bend. She was an alien it seemed.
She would always be. Her mind was too open.
Her spirit was too free.

Rebel

She was born with a rebel heart that beat to a rhythm few understood. She stuck out and didn't fit in. She often wished she could remain silent, but found it impossible amongst the lies. She had a voice that would not be silent. She had a spirit that would not conform. She had a will that would never yield.

Night Writer

The dark vastness of the night sky wrapped itself around her like a black blanket with rhinestone stars. The magnetic lunar pull that controlled the tides illuminated her mind, drawing it out of the fog. She sat fingertips to keys worn of their letters, stringing words, creating illusions, and escaping reality.

Windows and Orphans

Windows and orphans
Leave them not,
Be perfect,
So you must.

Running headers and rivers,
You'll never be
One of them
You can trust.

You're too crazy
Or perhaps lazy;
In all possibility,
You're just weird.

Who cares what they think,
They don't know how you sink
And fight with your pen
Things they've never feared.

I Am

There's that look that comes across their faces when I speak of things to which they cannot relate, and again I feel like some alien in human form.

I don't know why I see and feel the way I do, but it is clear to me that it is not a vantage point shared by many.

I feel like a freak, odd and alone. I know only a few will truly understand what it is I've been trying to say.

I have always been aware of my inability to fit in. I refuse to be anything but what I am for their comfort.

Outsider

She wasn't like them. She had tried to fit in, but somehow, she always found herself on the outside. It wasn't until she realized she was supposed to see things differently did she begin to enjoy the view.

Erased by the Darkness

Not long after midnight, I went outdoors. The night sky was filled with stars, the wind was brisk, and the wind chimes sang in the night air. I felt more peace in those moments than I had all day.

There was nothing in the darkness that frightened me. There was nothing under that black, glittering sky that caused my mind to weigh heavy. There was nothing in that air that caused me to feel sorrow. There was nothing but nature, in all her glory, and all her healing bliss.

I wanted to stay out there. I wanted to roam about like a nocturnal creature, safe in the shadows, at peace under the night sky, and soothed by the wind in my hair.

I am weary of all that does not bring me peace. If I could have kept for eternity the feeling I had while I was outdoors, I would have walked into the night to be erased by the darkness.

Mistaken

Life mistook my heart for a pin cushion.
Heartache, sorrow, loss—there are all sorts of
pins. Each pricked my heart.

Life mistook my mind for a dumping ground.
Happy, sad, horrifying—there are all kinds of
thoughts. Each cluttered my head.

Life mistook my soul for a ghost. Lost, cold,
forgotten—there are different kinds of ghosts.
Each haunted my existence.

The Condition

She was born with the condition—the condition of a mind that cannot stop thinking, and a heart that cannot stop feeling. She frequented the trenches of the war known as the human experience. She often heard the voices that whispered their suffering and sorrows. Try as she may, she could not stop seeing, hearing, and feeling their pain.

Passing of the Petals

Life is like petals
On a flower,
Beautiful
Until it fades.

One by one they fall,
Each passing moment
Until
It ceases to be.

Slowly it becomes
Nothing at all,
As if
It never existed,

Yet the memories
Echo eternally,
Haunting
The next life.

Endlessness

I felt life writhing in a warm, dark place. I drifted, lost in my thoughts, drowning in my feelings. Time crept up behind me and took me by surprise. The somber and sobering experience of mortality whispered.

The silence echoed a faint, memorable sound, both haunting and heartbreaking, like a child that softly whimpers and cannot be consoled.

The days drag on empty and cold when you're not here. Time becomes a jagged-edged blade, tearing my flesh, leaving an ugly scar that is long remembered.

Straight Through

She looked deeply into everything. She often saw things others did not. There was simplicity in complexity. She knew how to look past the busy patterns, through the intricate distractions, and see the simple truth.

Sunsets in Hell

The sinking feeling of depression creeps up on me again. It feels like a lead weight I've suddenly found myself encumbered with. Like an anchor, I toss it overboard. It swiftly sinks through the depths of the cold darkness and I along with it, yet I remain in the vessel from which it was dropped. A piece of me here, a piece of me there—all to keep the vessel in which I reside from drifting out to sea, forever to be lost.

I remain anchored in the vast ocean where the water meets the sky. I watch as the vibrant colors of the sunset reflect in the rippling salt water. The view is such that I am distracted from my suffering. I find myself in awe of the magnificent display of beauty in an existence that knows such anguish.

Perhaps one must suffer in some way. Perhaps one must feel the burden of one's anchor so that it will be tossed overboard, keeping one's vessel from being lost in the sea of life. Perhaps hell is not a place of eternal damnation and torment, but a place of learning and evolving. Perhaps what we call hell is simply the condition of being human.

The Company of Ghosts

Dawn swiftly approached. The dark, peaceful cover of night was fading, and soon she would find herself blinded by the harsh light of morning. The memories that haunted her refused to leave. She would spend another day with their ghosts.

Pieces

I tried to remember when I became so broken. I searched my memory for the moment—the event—that left me with fractures I couldn't mend no matter how hard I tried. As I sifted through memories, it occurred to me that none were powerful enough on their own to cause all the pieces I felt rattling within.

I called off the search with a sigh. There was no one specific thing, no catastrophic event that left me with these pieces. Instead it was a series of events that applied pressure, like the elements take their toll on a cement statue. Some left worn spots, others left cracks, while some took pieces.

I noticed the people I saw that day. I wondered how many pieces each had rattling about inside. Were there slowly chipped away, or were they shattered by one tragic blow?

How strong is the human spirit? How fragile is the human psyche? How much pressure does it take to break off pieces? I suppose it depends on the person. But one thing I am fairly certain of is we are all walking around with pieces. Those who don't rattle are just better at hiding their pain.

Unseen

It was still in all ways
Thorough many days—
A perpetual way to be.

It was silent in all places
So many faces—
Why do they keep looking at me?

I'm invisible, don't they know?
I left long ago—
They look, but they don't see.

Masking and Unveiling

She choked on secrets and was weighed down with stories. If they passed her lips they would stain. She chose each word with care and they became like a mask. Behind the mask she was silent, yet heard. Because of the mask she was invisible, yet seen.

Nil

I'm breaking,
Little pieces of me
Crumbling away,
Turning to dust
That covers
Everything.

A fine powder
Of sorrow—
Nothing can shine,
Nothing can be seen,
No one can hear me
Screaming.

Place of the Dead

Everything had become flat, flat and stagnant. I felt as if I was dying in someway—in all ways—and I wasn't sure I'd be able to save myself. I wasn't sure I wanted to. In many ways I already felt dead. In some respects, it felt as if I were a walking corpse.

I went to the place of the dead with my pen, notebook, and thoughts. I chose a spot under a large tree and sat on the grass. It was a beautiful summer day, not too hot, and there was a lovely breeze. I opened my notebook, took my pen, and spilled my thoughts onto paper.

In the shade of the tree, in the place of the dead, I felt better than I had all day. Something soothed me. Maybe it was the feeling of my bare feet and legs on the grass, connecting to the energy of the earth. Maybe it was the summer breeze dancing through my hair. Maybe it was the peaceful quiet of the cemetery with only the sounds of distant cars gently whooshing past and birds twittering.

My thoughts were interrupted when a pale-yellow spider crawled across my leg. The sensation of its legs tickling my skin startled me. The feeling confirmed I was still very much alive. I brushed the little spider off my leg with the back of my hand. I didn't mind spiders, as long as they didn't crawl on me.

I paused to read what I had written. After I skimmed the pages filled with my barely legible handwriting, I opened a bottle of seltzer water. It fizzed over the top and the cool, clear bubbly fluid dripped onto my legs. I looked around admiring the surroundings as I drank. Plush green grass, lovely old trees and headstones met my eyes as a one-word thought entered my mind: Freedom.

Why, I silently asked myself, had I thought of freedom in a place where they bury the dead? Perhaps because they were now free, the departed souls—free of the bounds of the human condition.

I sat there writing in the place of the dead, ink in my notebook and on my skin, and tried to remember why life was worth living.

Child of the Darkness

With a poison pen she had taken the hearts of many. Her ink was her blood, and it was as cryptic as her soul. Darkness hovered the night she was born, suspending her first breath until it claimed her as its own.

Charged

It crept up on her like a thief that stole something irreplaceable. She was left emotionally numb and physically trembling from the assault of her own mind.

Emotions could be powerful things, and she had the misfortune of generating such power. She was an energy bank of feelings. Each deposit left her heart heavy and her mind swirling.

The War Within

I choose the music for it is my mood that dominates. I cannot tolerate music that doesn't mirror my state of mind. There is already enough war within.

The battle rages on. My thoughts are holding my emotions hostage. They'll be released for a price, but I've nothing left to barter.

The air is thick and sticky, and it reeks of madness. My mind weighs heavy, but my heart is heavier, and it keeps sinking.

I take a deep breath and look at the sky. I watch a puffy, white cloud turn dark and ominous. I feel a smile attempt to cross my face. I like it when the weather reflects my mood.

It's just another day in my mind, where dark clouds roll in, where the music is somber, and where the war presses on. It will be a fight to the death. Surrendering is not an option.

Stained

Down you go
Ever so slow,
Hold on if you can.

It's quite sad,
You once had
Some sort of plan.

But now the voices
Are making choices,
Like lead you sink.

With blood you've tried,
To appease and abide,
Fingers stained with ink.

Abstract Art of the Insane

A bullet to the brain is just what the doctor ordered. He's not an ethical man, but he knows how to solve a problem...permanently.

I thought painting the walls with the contents of my head might be considered a revolting act, but then again, it might be art...depending on the blood splatter pattern, of course. It would be abstract art, naturally, the medium: blood, brain matter, and skull fragments.

I walked about the house looking for a wall for my pending artwork, but found myself sighing in each room. There wasn't a free wall to be found. I pondered removing the framed photos and paintings from one of the walls, thereby revealing a blank canvas, but the phone rang. I answered it.

It was death. My heart quickened. Blank canvas or not, perhaps I would be creating that abstract artwork after all. Death put me on hold. I waited apprehensively, impatiently, frustratingly. I heard a click and then the dial tone. Apparently, death had another call.

Living Things

She knew what it was meant to be, but could not help noticing all that it actually was. She dissected life like a biology student with a frog pinned to a tray, its soft underside exposed to her sharp scrutiny.

Oddly Fashioned

She drifted from place to place never really fitting in anywhere. She was an oddly fashioned being with darkness in her mind and light in her soul. She never expected to be understood by many, but perhaps by a few.

Altered State

Escape
You know how,
Sleep
Forget your concerns—

Dream
The alternate state,
Reality
Twists and turns—

Wake
Time is illusion,
Accept
Being conscious burns.

Dreams of Freedom

She drifted with the waves as the tide ebbed and flowed. She felt a peace come over her, and she let go. Deep into the cool, dark water she sank, unencumbered and free.

The Dark Side

It's sharp and twisted,
This consuming thought;
I've bled many words,
Was it for naught?

I'm striving for balance,
But it keeps insisting
I open my veins,
Yet I keep resisting.

The sorrow is so binding,
Few find their way free;
The dark side is calling,
I must answer its plea.

Madness and Mayhem

It is all that it is and all that it is not, and that would be enough. It would never be understood, not completely, but that no longer mattered.

The fury had reared its head, and the depth of the darkness had come along for the ride. Together there would be madness and mayhem. Blood wouldn't be enough. Suffering wouldn't be enough. Complete destruction is the only thing that would do.

I smiled at death for I knew how utterly misunderstood it was. It was not the end. It was the beginning, and how I longed to begin, yet again, and find my way free from this moment.

The lifetimes, the misery, the endless repeating of lessons only to fail to learn them well enough, to have to do it all over again—this is what we called living.

The people, the same souls with different faces, and how we kept dancing that waltz—how we all seemed to remember the steps, and how we loved and hated one another equally.

The brilliance that lies sleeping in the madness that must remain hidden. How well do I act my part? How well do I keep my mask in place as I twirl about the stage?

If I were to fall in all my twirling, and my head were to be cracked open like the shell of an egg, out would ooze the yolk that encased words and scramble them you must...for they are no good unless consumed, and no good consumed unless properly prepared.

One that is deep is deep enough to drown in. Dive in and swim down to the darkest parts, where the light never reaches, past the point where you can no longer hold your breath, and try to remember.

Blood truly is thicker than water, and it's much harder to drink. The warmth of the sun can become the cold of the darkness. Madness is a fickle state, and mayhem knows no mercy.

It was everything and nothing. That is all. That is all.

Conquering the Conjuring

She was a creature of the darkness, but some things in the shadows plagued her. She faced them, accepted them, and remained amongst them. She emerged, still a creature of the darkness, but filled with a light that illuminated what the darkness could conjure.

Mindfully Mad

Pain had served its purpose.
Blood had served as ink.
She had hushed the voices
That drove her to the brink.

The edge of insanity,
She balanced on its ledge;
A precarious existence
With a razor-sharp edge.

Everything and Nothing

She felt as if she had one foot in reality and the other in some distant realm. Perhaps it was the realm of the dead. Perhaps she was merely at a crossroads.

She remained strong yet fragile, heard yet silent, seen yet invisible, here yet gone. She was but part of the collective imagination, yet so vividly real, one could hear her echoes sifting through the sands of time.